Original title:
Petals and Patience

Copyright © 2025 Creative Arts Management OÜ
All rights reserved.

Author: Maya Livingston
ISBN HARDBACK: 978-1-80581-874-8
ISBN PAPERBACK: 978-1-80581-401-6
ISBN EBOOK: 978-1-80581-874-8

The Quiet Path to Blooming Colors

In the garden, a snail moves slow,
Comparing itself to a rushing crow.
With every inch, it turns to muse,
Baking thoughts of floral views.

A daisy told a rose to chill,
"You know, we both got time to thrill!"
The sunflower danced with glee so bright,
Swaying to the left, then to the right.

Bumblebees in tuxedos fuss,
Wondering why they ride the bus.
"Pollinate or bust; no time to fret,"
They argue while fetching their honey bet.

Laughter loud from petals near and far,
As violets host a garden bazaar.
With jokes about a leaf's bad hair day,
They flutter and giggle, come what may.

The Unfurling of Soft Lights

In the garden where flowers gossip,
One thinks night is much hotter than a fish.
They wear gowns of color, like a bad prom night,
But who'll tell them they look quite delish?

A bee buzzed by with a loud, silly dance,
As roses rolled their eyes like they were keen.
Ruffled petals held secrets of romance,
While daisies pleaded, "Just keep it between!"

Nature's Unwavering Faithfulness

The oak tree sighs with the weight of its jokes,
While squirrels take bets on who'll win the race.
The daisies giggle, playing silly folks,
Oh, the puns that drift all over the place!

Worms in the soil host a comedy show,
With punchlines that tickle the roots down below.
Sunshine beams in and gives us a wink,
Nature must think we're all quite on the brink!

Growing Dreams in Mellow Light

The sun dips low, with a wink and a nod,
While shadows sway like dancers in a club.
The dreams stretching soft, like a well-fed cod,
Combine with laughter in a plant-based pub.

Earthworms bicker, who'll dig deeper than the rest?
While crickets chirp jokes about stars in their nests.
Every bloom finds a way to break into song,
Even when nature's humor goes a bit wrong!

Silent Storms of Petal Softness

Hushed whispers curl in the evening's light,
Tickling the leaves in a playful ballet.
The flowers compete for the title of bright,
As rain begs for the chance to join in their play.

Storms shake and rattle, all flowers take cover,
While frogs in their coats croak their worst pick-up lines.
It's a riot of nature, such chaos to uncover,
It's cloudy with laughter and sunshine designs!

The Rhythm of Slow Unfolding

In a garden where clocks are shy,
Flowers dance while bees buzz by.
With each tick, they take their time,
Like toddlers learning to rhyme.

Sunlight spills like laughter's song,
Every moment, nothing feels wrong.
Nature's ballet, slow and sweet,
Even snails find joy in their feet.

Cultivating Dreams in Dewy Mornings

Morning dew embraces the grass,
As squirrels hold philosophical class.
Dreams sprout like daisies in bloom,
While the rooster sends out a boom.

Coffee grounds sing a sleepy tune,
While bumblebees chase the moon.
In this hum of warm delight,
Even dreams get sleepy at night.

A Canvas of Time and Tenderness

Brush strokes made of sun and cheer,
Art creates a scene right here.
With time, each color finds its way,
As butterflies come out to play.

A painter's laugh, a gentle tease,
Makes the canvas dance with ease.
In every shade, a giggle hides,
As the breeze becomes our guide.

The Elegant Expression of Desire

Hearts twirl like dancers in a jest,
Chasing dreams in a carefree quest.
With a wink and a little grin,
They leap into the mess within.

Puppies tug at all the strings,
In the chaos, love just sings.
Every blush, a cheerful shout,
Life's a game we can't live without.

Whispers of Blooming Grace

In gardens where the daisies droop,
A snail is plotting quite the loop.
With every inch, he takes his time,
While bumblebees are on a climb.

The flowers giggle in the breeze,
As ants all gather for the tease.
Each bloom is dressed in colors bright,
While grasshoppers prepare for flight.

A worm recites a silly verse,
All while the sun plays with the purse.
The petals laugh and swish around,
In this small world, joy can be found.

So here's to those who take things slow,
These tiny folks with hearts aglow.
If you can wait like a wise old tree,
You'll find humor blooming, just like me.

The Dance of Serenity

The wind arrives with giggles low,
A flower twirls—a lovely show.
While squirrels dance on tiny toes,
The daisies play the funny pros.

In sunshine's glow, the bees all hum,
While ladybugs make quite the drum.
A butterfly flutters, seeking laughs,
As the sun sneaks peek through the halves.

But oh, the tulips wear a frown,
They envy all the jokers 'round.
Yet in their stubborn stance, they learn,
To smile and shift, with grace they yearn.

The daffodils, with radiant pride,
Invite us all to join the ride.
So take a step, and sway along,
In nature's queue, we all belong.

Fragments of a Gentle Spring

The crocus pops from winter's sleep,
It peeks around, then starts to weep.
The clouds above take on some cheer,
As springtime spreads, it's finally here.

The rabbits race, a sight to see,
While turtles yawn, sipping their tea.
A robin sings a merry score,
While blossoms giggle at the door.

The sunbeams slip through leafy beams,
Chasing shadows, brightening dreams.
Yet dandelions plot a scheme,
To grow all wild, a giggling team.

In every bloom, a smile is cast,
Each blossom knows that joy can last.
So sow your seeds, and watch them grow,
For laughter thrives where flowers glow.

When Blooms Embrace Time

In the garden, clovers chat away,
They glimpse the sun at break of day.
With puddles jumping like they know,
The jokes they tell, they steal the show.

The lilacs blush and start to sway,
As bumblebees ask, 'What's your play?'
Their honey jars are full of dreams,
While sunlight dances on the beams.

The daisies quip, 'We're here to stay,'
While cacti chuckle, come what may.
Each flower knows, with time so sweet,
That laughter makes their lives complete.

So take a seat amid the greens,
And join the fun, whatever it means.
In blooms and laughs, let's intertwine,
With nature's grace, we'll sip on thyme.

A Journey Through Unseen Changes

In a garden where daisies play,
A snail decides to run today.
He races past a sleeping bee,
Who dreams of honey, wild and free.

With every bloom, the bugs all cheer,
The ladybug lost in her mirror,
She's convinced she's the queen of grace,
Yet trips on dew, now what a chase!

A worm is teaching leaves to dance,
While ants hold conferences by chance,
They're plotting who will steal the show,
But stumble on a shadow's glow.

Tommy Toad gets up to sing,
While frogs all laugh at his old string,
He croaks a tune most out of line,
Yet all agree he's quite divine!

Revelations Hidden in the Quiet

In the hush where daisies nod,
A squirrel plans to beat the odds,
He bets his acorns on a race,
But ends up with seed stuck on his face.

The quiet blooms with silly sounds,
As bunnies hop on garden rounds,
Their laughter echoes pure delight,
While flowers blush in morning light.

A caterpillar tells jokes to flies,
They roll in laughter, oh what a prize,
Yet right on cue, they lose their wings,
And ponder why the humor stings.

A hidden gnome keeps watchful eyes,
As garden creatures brave their tries,
With patience, they will find the way,
To dance and laugh another day!

The Silent Promise of Spring

Beneath the frost, a secret stirs,
The crocuses chuckle, then it purrs,
They plot to burst out at first light,
While snowflakes schwack, "This isn't right!"

In the chill, the ants arrange,
A convention to discuss the change,
They're all excited, plans abound,
Till one forgot to come around.

A feeble sun peeks through the fog,
And bumps into a lazy frog,
"Let's hop and sing, it's time to play!"
But frog responds with a snooze all day.

The brook giggles as it flows,
Tickling rocks in funny prose,
While frogs recite their morning tales,
Echoing laughter, nature prevails!

Whispers in the Wind's Embrace

In the breeze where secrets hide,
The flowers gossip and confide,
They swap their stories, sly and fun,
While butterflies plot to take a run.

The wind stirs up a silly game,
As petals swirl like wide-eyed fame,
A dandelion dares to dance,
But lands in soup—oh, what a chance!

A crafty fox runs through the trees,
But trips on roots, followed by bees,
They giggle low but can't outrun,
For nature's jokes are always fun.

As sunlight fades, the critters cheer,
Playing chase till night draws near,
In whispers soft, they share delight,
Beneath the stars, all feels just right!

The Unseen Journey of the Heart

In a garden where laughter lies,
Silly thoughts begin to rise.
A snail races a cheerful flame,
Both claiming they will win the game.

With every twist and every turn,
A dance of joy, we start to learn.
Now bumpers of a butterfly,
Awkward, but they still can fly.

Tickling breezes tease the ground,
While whispers of delight abound.
A shy rose blushes in the breeze,
With giggles from the buzzing bees.

Love's a journey, slow and sweet,
Like finding socks with mismatched feet.
So we wander, with a grin,
Even if the race won't begin.

A Love Letter to Unhurried Days

Oh, how I cherish lazy hours,
When time meanders like wild flowers.
Even the clock seems to conspire,
To let us lounge beside the fire.

The sun takes naps, it seems so fair,
While we exchange our idle stares.
In mismatched pajamas, we find delight,
As the world spins on, in sheer delight.

Tea spills over, oh what a mess,
The cat steals my scone, I confess.
Yet laughter flows, a gentle stream,
Carving joy from the wildest dream.

Like butter on a warm, soft roll,
These unhurried days stay in control.
Life's too funny to rush or race,
We'll savor sweetness, at our pace.

Dreams Seeded in Twilight's Glow

At dusk, when whispers softly tease,
The stars giggle behind the trees.
We toss our wishes to the sky,
And watch the clouds as they float by.

With hopes as light as dandelion fluff,
We gather dreams, oh, just enough.
A wishbone steals the show tonight,
Pulling pranks, oh what a sight!

As shadows blend in playful ways,
We dance on sidewalks, lost in haze.
Laughter blooms in every nook,
Our dreams are sneaky, like a book.

So here's to twilight's playful flight,
Where dreams take off into the night.
With smiles as big as the moon's bright face,
We find our dreams in this silly space.

The Poise of the Unseen

With grace, the unseen takes the lead,
Like a duck that's wearing bloomers, indeed!
It waddles with a royal air,
While we just giggle and stand there.

A quiet whimsy shapes our way,
In every corner, come what may.
Like socks that vanish in the wash,
We laugh at fate's absurd little posh.

The subtle hints of joy and glee,
Creep in like ants at a picnic spree.
With every hiccup, life's a jest,
Full of quirks, we know the rest.

So let's embrace the weird and wild,
Like a giggling, mischief-making child.
In the unspoken moments that we miss,
Lies the gentle nudge of sweet abyss.

The Blossoming Hour

In the garden, bees do dance,
They tickle flowers, not a chance.
With every buzz, they lose their way,
A silly game they love to play.

Buds are laughing, color bright,
Fluttering wings in pure delight.
They tease the blooms, a floral jest,
In this garden, who is best?

Roots are tangled, like bad jokes,
Laughing soil, with joyful pokes.
As seeds sprout soft, and grace the air,
Even worms can't help but stare.

So let us pause, enjoy the view,
Nature's humor, fresh and new.
For every bloom that comes to light,
There's laughter hidden, pure and bright.

Inhaled Hues of Hope

Colors swirl like silly dreams,
Dancing bright in sunlight's beams.
A violet giggles with delight,
As daisies wear their hats just right.

Chasing rainbows, a playful race,
Brushes painting every face.
With splashes of yellow and bold green,
Laughter sprouts, a vibrant scene.

The sun sneezes, a beam of glee,
A chuckle shared with every bee.
The clouds giggle, float on by,
A silly sky, where colors fly.

Breath in colors, let them spread,
Brighten up your sleepy head.
For in the hues of joy we find,
A world that's funny, kind, and blind.

Soft Murmurs of the Earth

The earth whispers in the spring,
A funny sigh from underground bling.
With tiny giggles, roots explore,
They play hide-and-seek, who's keeping score?

Worms get tangled in their thread,
Dreaming big of the life ahead.
While ladybugs wear polka dots,
Stirring laughter in small plots.

Grass blades sway, a gentle tease,
They tickle toes, go where they please.
As ants march in their silly lines,
Life's a dance, with quirky signs.

So let's listen to the ground,
In funny whispers, joy is found.
For every murmur shared with glee,
Is nature's way, wild and free.

Cultivating Dreams in the Garden

In the garden, plans take flight,
Seeds that giggle under moonlight.
They dream of being flowers, oh so bold,
But yell at weeds who just won't fold!

Squirrels plotting with acorns near,
Making mischief while we cheer.
With every dig and tiny toss,
A raucous bloom turns into gloss!

Tending dreams with dirty hands,
It's a funny mess across the lands.
While butterflies plot their spring parade,
Gardeners laugh in sun and shade.

Planting smiles, our work is light,
With nature's humor, hearts take flight.
For in this space, where dreams are sown,
A garden's laughter feels like home.

A Symphony of Fading Light

In twilight's dance, we twirl and sway,
With shadows chasing the light away.
Laughter echoes in the air,
As fireflies join, without a care.

A crabby frog sits on a log,
He croaks complaints to every dog.
The moon winks down with a silly grin,
While night unfolds, let the fun begin!

A breeze sends leaves into a whirl,
And everyone gives their best twirl.
The stars above giggle and tease,
While crickets play out melodies with ease.

As darkness spreads its cozy cape,
The world's a stage, a grand escape.
In fading light, we frolic still,
Moments of joy, a laughter spill.

Unseen Forces of Nature's Will

The wind yells loud, a playful beast,
It brings the leaves, a swirling feast.
Squirrels scamper, no time to chatter,
As acorns fall, and watch them scatter.

The ants parade, like tiny kings,
Carrying crumbs and other things.
While clouds make faces, oh-so-round,
And raindrops laugh as they hit the ground.

A butterfly sneezes, then takes flight,
It leads the way through the sunny light.
The flowers giggle, sway to the tune,
In this wacky dance, beneath the moon.

Nature's tricks are full of cheer,
Invisible strings that pull us near.
With laughter and fun, the day unfolds,
In nature's embrace, we're never too old.

The Quiet Craft of Becoming

In a cozy nook, new dreams are born,
Where thoughts expand like a comfy yarn.
Busy hands sculpt with a gentle touch,
In hushed whispers, creating much.

The paintbrush jigs, like it's got a goal,
Swinging and swaying while I take a stroll.
My canvas giggles, "Add a splash here!"
And the colors dance without any fear.

Time tiptoes by, but that's just fine,
As I mix my blues with a bit of wine.
Oh! A masterpiece, or so I declare,
A glorious mess, with splatters everywhere!

In secret corners of my own mind,
Imagination tumbles, playful and kind.
The quiet craft, a joyful tease,
Where laughter lives and worries freeze.

In the Heart of Waiting Gardens

In waiting gardens, time stands still,
Where daisies plot their sneaky thrill.
With worms that wiggle, digging deep,
They dream of secrets they won't keep.

Sunshine giggles, tickling blooms,
As bunnies hop around in costumes.
Each flower whispers, "Let's play today!"
While butterflies flutter in a ballet.

The soil chuckles, rich with tales,
Of muddy boots and funny fails.
The rain joins in, a drumroll sound,
As nature's circus spins around.

Patience reigns in this green ballet,
With roots entwined in a grand display.
Through gentle waits, laughs bloom anew,
In gardens where joy is always in view.

The Anticipation of Honeyed Hours

A bee buzzed by with glee,
It danced around a giant tree.
Thought it found a sugary sack,
But ended up on a turtle's back.

The sun climbed high, the sky so blue,
The flowers laughed, their colors true.
Each day they bloomed, so bright, so loud,
While bees just slept under a cloud.

The breeze blew soft, with whispers sweet,
While ants marched on, a patterned beat.
They dreamed of feasts on summer's eve,
While all the flowers rolled their leaves.

But soon the sky turned gray and dark,
And every critter lost its spark.
Yet still we wait for sun's return,
For honeyed hours, our hearts still yearn.

The Lullaby of Earth and Air

A dandelion found a friend,
A wayward seed that had to mend.
It wished to fly and roam about,
But landed in a cat's meow-out.

The trees sang low, a sleepy tune,
While sleepy bees stuck to the bloom.
An ant declared, with all his might,
"Let's nap away this lazy light!"

The clouds drifted, a hushed parade,
As flowers snoozed in fragrant shade.
But in the night, stars tickled low,
Making ticklish dreams for those below.

Yet all must wake, as mornings do,
The story turns, and so we flew.
With every laugh, we see what's near,
In funny ways, the world appears!

Murmurs of Nature's Timelessness

A squirrel chattered in a hurry,
While mushrooms' caps began to curry.
The wind it giggled, trees did sway,
Nature's whispers, always in play.

Each raindrop fell with clumsy grace,
Making ponds for a frog's embrace.
He croaked a tune, not quite on key,
But all the flowers danced with glee.

A fox debated with a hare,
Who'd race faster? A classic flair!
The sun just rolled its golden eyes,
As critters argued under the skies.

But hours pass, and laughter flows,
In every nook where wild things grow.
From silent roots to skyward height,
Nature's jesters, a pure delight!

A Palette of Patient Wishes

A painter sat under the sun,
With colors bright, she called it fun.
Each brush stroke swirled in wind's embrace,
A canvas danced, lost in its grace.

The flowers posed, they struck a stance,
While bees attempted a wobbly dance.
They tipped and tumbled, fell in bloom,
Creating chaos, spilling perfume.

A ladybug joined for the show,
With winged flair, she stole the glow.
The painter laughed, her smile was wide,
In every flick, her heart confides.

As day turned night, her palette glowed,
With wishes wrapped in dreams bestowed.
In every color, a tale unfurls,
While giggles paint the universe's curls.

Beneath the Surface of Stillness

In a pond where frogs play tricks,
The water's calm hides their little flicks.
A splash, a croak, oh what a show,
As lily pads pretend to grow.

Squirrels plotting from on high,
Chasing shadows, oh me, oh my!
Each jump is quite a daring feat,
While laughing leaves join in the beat.

A turtle at the edge takes a nap,
Dreaming dreams of a snack-filled trap.
The stillness holds a secret joke,
As a wise old heron smirks then spoke.

For in the quiet, life's absurd,
Each tiny flutter, a comical word.
Beneath the calm, the chaos sings,
In nature's play, oh the joy it brings.

The Gentleness of Eased Souls

Two butterflies with goofy grace,
Dance in air, what a silly race!
With wobbly turns and flappy spins,
Their flight is where the laughter begins.

A gentle breeze starts to tease,
It sways the flowers, makes them sneeze.
Pollen springs like confetti bright,
The garden's party is full of light.

A ladybug lost on a spree,
Waves to a bug, but it's just a tree.
"Hey, you with the green shiny bark!"
He rolls his eyes, "Not quite the spark."

In the gentle hum of the day,
Life's silly mix leads the way.
With every laugh, a soul finds cheer,
In the soft embrace that's always near.

A Tapestry Woven in Time

Threads of laughter snub the loom,
In every stitch, there's space to zoom.
A quirky quilt made of silly yarn,
Where patchwork critters wail and barn.

Grandma's cat, with a swagger proud,
Found the fabric and bowed to the crowd.
Rolling around in a fabric schnauze,
While grandpa chuckled, "What a rouse!"

In every fold, a secret hides,
Where goofy tales of folly bides.
A tapestry that sways and swirls,
With echoes of fantastical whirls.

So here's to life's jumbled design,
A mix of moments, both yours and mine.
With laughter woven through each line,
We find a rhythm, simply divine!

The Serenity of Future Blossoms

Underneath the skies so wide,
Flowers plot their secret glide.
With winks and nudges, they conspire,
To bloom in hues that will inspire.

A sunflower tips its hat with flair,
To clouds floating by without a care.
"Have you seen the bees?" it jokes with glee,
"They're buzzing loud in a silly spree!"

Dandelions laugh at the breeze's tease,
Prancing around like they own the trees.
With each puff, they send seeds in flight,
A comet of wishes in the soft twilight.

So here's to blooms yet to appear,
With colors that sparkle and bring us cheer.
In the garden where giggles frolic and play,
Serenity waits, hip-hip-hooray!

The Role of Time in Nature's Theater

In nature's grand old play, they twirl,
The daisies giggle, the wind gives a whirl.
A snail takes a bow, it moves so slow,
While frogs in tuxedos steal the show.

The trees start to gossip, leaves in a dance,
Winking at sunbeams, they take a chance.
A squirrel forgets where it buried a nut,
Shrugging it off, "Oops, that's just my rut!"

Like clocks that tick softly, they know the score,
Finding humor in moments, who'd ask for more?
The sun and the moon, they're a bit of a tease,
Swapping their hats whenever they please.

Each season a joke, each bloom a pun,
Even the rain seems to have its fun.
The world spins around in this hilarious scheme,
Nature's theater, a wild daydream.

Moments Cradled in Gentle Hands

A baby bird chirps, in a cozy clutch,
Its dreams are as silly as a teddy bear's touch.
With a blink and a wiggle, it takes to the air,
Owls giggle softly, while fixing their hair.

In the garden, a weed throws a wild party,
Dancing with daisies, being quite hearty.
The bees hum a tune, slightly out of tune,
While butterflies twirl beneath the full moon.

A worm in the soil joins the fun in style,
Rolling and wriggling, a summer's fake smile.
Time giggles along, a mischievous tease,
Reminding us all, it's okay to be free.

So let's cradle each moment with laughter and light,
Like fireflies flickering through warm summer nights.
With gentle hands grasping life's wacky sway,
Who knew a flower could be so cliché?

Dreams Yet to Unfold

A dandelion puffs out a wish in the breeze,
Chasing dreams lightly, like kids with no keys.
With a pop and a giggle, they float up so high,
The wishes are dancing; who knows where they fly?

A caterpillar chuckles, "I'm destined to soar,
Just give me a moment; I'll open the door."
Stuck in a cocoon, it wiggles in place,
Imagining wings in this awkward embrace.

Every seed has a story, a plan yet unclear,
Sprouting in silence, that's how dreams appear.
So why rush the journey or fuss about fate?
Each moment's a chapter, don't worry, just wait.

When fruits finally ripen, they'll burst with a grin,
A journey more joyful than where it's been.
So let the dreams flutter, and let the time slide,
In nature's grand circus, we'll all take a ride.

The Delicate Anatomy of Longing

A rose waits and sighs, for a bee to arrive,
Longing for company, it starts to thrive.
But what if the bee is out on a spree,
Flirting with flowers, being wildly free?

The tulips are blushing, they're dressed quite prim,
"Why's love so picky?" they mutter on whim.
With petals a-flutter and pollen on the side,
They practice sweet lines while the wind is their guide.

The moon leans in close, whispers tales of the night,
The stars are attentive, all twinkling with light.
In the garden of yearning, the heart plays a game,
Proposing to daisies, yet none knows their name.

So here blooms affection, a humorous scheme,
Comparing ourselves to a long, silly dream.
In the dance of desire, we're all just so bold,
Finding laughter in longing—let the story unfold.

Echoes of Nature's Calm

In the garden, bees do dance,
Humming tunes, giving flowers a chance.
Yet I find them quite the tease,
Buzzing by as I plant my peas.

The sun's a ball, bright and bold,
While squirrels plot, or so I'm told.
They race around, my seeds in tow,
Making mischief, putting on a show.

Worms have their parties underground,
With soil cakes and roots abound.
While I sip tea, they conspire,
To eat my lettuce, such quagmire!

A breeze will tickle, leaves will sway,
Nature's humor in full display.
With each laugh, my worries cease,
In this lively patch, I find my peace.

Heartbeats in the Garden

The daisies droop, they've had their fun,
While thorns just poke, oh what a run!
I dance around, as bugs take flight,
With every step, I trip in delight.

The daisies gossip, petals all askew,
"Who needs a gardener? Just look at you!"
They laugh and tease, they grow so tall,
While I bend low, in my best butterfly call.

A gopher giggles, peeking from his hole,
Declaring himself the garden's soul.
"Plant something green, or I'm outta here!"
Now I fear my greens may disappear.

As laughter flows, the flowers bloom,
Nature's antics light up the room.
With whimsy bright, and joy to share,
In this heart-shaped plot, we dance in air.

Threads of Color and Quiet

The paintbrush blooms in every hue,
But bees say, "That's old news, boo!"
With laughs and giggles, they take a spin,
Turning life's threads into a silly grin.

Sunflowers stand, all proud and tall,
While I trip over roots, oh what a sprawl!
"Hey there, buddy!" they chuckle loud,
"Stand up straight, it's time to be proud!"

The breeze comes through, a gentle tease,
Whispering secrets that float like bees.
Yet I'm left guessing, joining the game,
While butterflies flutter, and all look the same.

In this canvas of green, rainbow flowers sway,
Funny how nature brightens the day.
With giggles and joy, laughter takes flight,
In each tiny bud, there's unexpected delight.

The Language of Stillness

Invisible whispers echo the ground,
Nature's chuckles are all around.
Each little leaf, a jokester proud,
Making mischief, oh so loud!

The clouds roll by, wearing silly hats,
While ants debate in their tiny spats.
"Who's the fastest?" they shout and dart,
While I sit back, enjoying the art.

Rabbits bounce under the laughing trees,
Doing the tango, if you please!
With every jig, a flower sways,
In this quiet fun, joy fills the days.

Amongst the green, life's quirks intertwine,
Nature fabricates a punchline divine.
In stillness we find, with hearts intertwined,
The lightness of laughter, perfectly aligned.

Enchanted by Soft Fragrance

In the garden, bees do zoom,
Sipping nectar with a vroom.
They forget their buzzing race,
Just to find a flowery face.

A squirrel's dance, oh what a show,
Chasing leaves where soft winds blow.
Yet in all this merry plight,
Someone lost their nuts last night!

The sun above begins to laugh,
Casting shadows on my path.
A butterfly in silly spins,
Twirls as if it wears my sins.

With such a scene, I can't complain,
Laughter blooms like springtime rain.
Oh nature's humor, bright as day,
Keeps all my worries far at bay.

Beneath Layers of Color

Underneath the vibrant hues,
A wandering duck looks for shoes.
Waddle left, then waddle right,
Lost its way, as day turns night.

A painter spilled his whole delight,
Creating chaos with each bite.
Tubes of green are rolling fast,
Where's the canvas? Oh, it's past!

The flowers gossip, oh so sweet,
About the grass that dares to cheat.
While daisies stretch, trying to grow,
A lazy lark just steals the show.

Under the sun, oh what a sight,
Each bloom competes for pure delight.
With veggies plotting their big heist,
The garden laughs, it's brunch and feast.

Budding Dreams and Silent Wishes

A tiny seed begins to sprout,
"Where am I? There's too much clout!"
The worms debate on what to eat,
While grumpy soil calls for a treat.

Hoping for a sunny day,
One little leaf starts to sway.
A breeze whispers a gentle joke,
"Don't worry dear, you'll soon be woke!"

A ladybug with tiny specs,
Brags her spot is well complex.
"I'm more stylish than that rose!
Check my dots, just look and pose!"

Beneath the green, a laugh erupts,
As critters dream of all their ups.
In secret smiles, they twist and twine,
Planting hopes with a sip of wine.

The Calm After the Storm

After downpours come the glee,
Puddles form—a perfect spree.
Kids jump in with laughing shouts,
Splashing while the sunshine doubts.

A rainbow arches, proud and bold,
While clouds grumble, feeling old.
"Why'd you leave? We had some fun!"
They sigh and drip, but on they run.

A squirrel shakes off water drops,
Then mumbles as it makes its hops.
"Should have skipped that yesterday,
Now I'm soaked—oh, what a day!"

Yet joy abounds with every ray,
Hats are donned, it's time to play.
With every twinkle, laughter's near,
After the storm, it's all sincere.

The Unraveling of Nature's Tapestry

In gardens where the daisies dance,
The weeds declare their clumsy stance.
A ladybug in polka dots,
Thinks she's the queen of all the plots.

The sunbeam jokes with climbing vines,
While trees complain of twisted lines.
A hose sings out a silly tune,
As squirrels plot their afternoon.

Butterflies wear socks of stripes,
While ants march on with different types.
The flowers share their gossip bright,
In colors bold, a funny sight.

So when the blooms begin to sway,
Just know they're laughing all the way.
Nature's whimsy, full of cheer,
Keeps us amused throughout the year.

Beneath the Weight of Time

The clock sat on a crooked shelf,
Spinning tales of an old self.
Roses chuckled, 'What a fuss!'
While thorns just poked and rode the bus.

A snail, quite proud, took his sweet time,
While old oak trees played nursery rhyme.
The seconds ticked, the minutes mocked,
As nature's plan was overtocked.

A squirrel slid down a mossy chair,
And offered time a berry to share.
But time just winked and said, 'Not so!'
'I'm late for work; I have to go!'

Yet in the garden's gentle grace,
There's humor found in every space.
Where laughter grows and sunshine beams,
Life's a tapestry of silly dreams.

Silence Between the Colors

In hues of laughter, silence breaks,
Where rainbow leaves converse with flakes.
Each shade has secrets, keeps them tight,
While grinning grasshoppers hop in flight.

The blue whispers to the golden blooms,
About the sun's amusing zooms.
A violet giggles, 'What a jest!'
As colors play, they feel so blessed.

The palette spins in silly tangles,
While butterflies tease with their angles.
Painting jokes across the breeze,
Bringing smiles with crafty ease.

So let the shades collide and blend,
In every dip, let laughter send.
For silence blooms in shades of glee,
A canvas full of jubilee.

Vibrance in the Void

In shadows lurked a silly shade,
Where brightness whispered, 'Don't be afraid.'
A flower sprouted from the gloom,
Exclaiming, 'I've got lots of room!'

The night giggled with the stars up high,
While clouds played tag, oh my, oh my!
Each glimmer wore a goofy grin,
As the moon chortled, 'Join in the din!'

Hues danced around in chuckling jest,
While colors plotted their own fest.
Even the dusk with arms so wide,
Could not contain its silly pride.

So when the void seems deep, unkind,
Just look for joy, and you will find,
Vibrance lurks where laughter's bold,
In every corner, tales retold.

Colors Drifting Through Unhurried Days

In fields where daisies flirt and sway,
A bee named Bob got lost today.
He danced with blooms, a wild affair,
But tripped on grass without a care.

A butterfly with quite a flair,
Wore polka dots, but thought it rare.
It swooped and twirled in sunny glee,
While Bob kept stepping on a bee!

The sunbeams giggled in delight,
As Bob gave chase, with all his might.
But every time he took a leap,
Those flowers laughed! They didn't keep.

So, under skies so vast and blue,
The dance of joy began anew.
A world so bright, with all its bloom,
Where humor waits in nature's room.

The Longing of Green Tendrils

Tendrils reaching, oh so spry,
A vine named Charlie waved goodbye.
He missed the fence that held him tight,
And now he climbed, to everyone's fright!

He found a hat up in a tree,
And thought, perhaps, it's meant for he.
So on he leapt, with all his zeal,
Straight to the brim—oh, what a meal!

The neighbors watched with wide-eyed glee,
"A vine, a hat, what can it be?"
Charlie chuckled in the breeze,
"Perhaps I'm just a leafy tease!"

With every twist, he waved hello,
To every passerby, a show.
In gardens green, where laughter clings,
Who knew a vine could sprout such things?

Layered Shades of Hope

In a patch of colors, bold and bright,
A rabbit danced with pure delight.
He leaped through shades of yellow and blue,
While critters laughed at his hoppy view.

"Oh, look at me!" he proudly yelled,
"I'm layered up, my fashion's held!"
But as he spun with all his flair,
His tail got caught in a lovely chair!

The daisies snickered, "Oh dear friend,
Your style's a hit, but what a bend!"
He wriggled free, then shook his fur,
And twirled again—a fuzzy blur!

Amidst the blooms, he found his groove,
Each layer shining, he had to move.
So in the flower-riddled glen,
The rabbit danced—oh, what a trend!

Between Moments, Beauty Blooms

Two ants debated where to roam,
"Let's find the sweets, we'll make it home!"
But one got caught in a sticky mess,
And shouted, "Help! I can't impress!"

The other laughed, "You're stuck, my mate!
Let's take a break and contemplate."
They sat on blades just like a throne,
With candy dreams and hopes well-known.

Along came a worm, with wit so sly,
"I'll help you out, just let me try!"
But twisted 'round, he got ensnared,
And joined the party, unprepared.

So here they sat, a trio bold,
With bugs and sweets, their stories told.
In nature's dance, where laughter swells,
Amongst the thorns, true friendship dwells.

Between Moments, Beauty Blooms

A wallflower stood, feeling quite shy,
While butterflies soared, oh my, oh my!
They dipped and dived, with such allure,
While she stayed planted, unsure and pure.

"Come join us here, it's fun!" they cried,
But she just shrank, with petals wide.
Then came a breeze, with gentle sway,
And lifted her up, without delay!

"Oh, wow!" she gasped, as she took flight,
No longer ground-bound, what a sight!
The butterflies cheered, "You're one of us now!
Let's dance in the sun, you'll learn just how!"

From shy beginnings, blooms took wing,
In moments shared, they'd laugh and sing.
So if you find yourself alone,
Just follow the wind—you'll find your home.

Unwind the Threads of Expectation

Twisting threads, they laugh and twirl,
Expectations spin in a merry whirl.
With every tug, a giggle grows,
As hopeful dreams play hide and show.

In the loom of time, they weave and tease,
The fabric of life, a quilt of ease.
With each stitch, a jest or jest,
To lighten hearts and make us rest.

Frogs wear crowns with silly grace,
As stitched-up plans dance in their place.
A puppet show of hopes and fates,
Beneath the fabric, laughter waits.

So unwind those threads, let joy ignite,
For each tangled knot brings pure delight.
In silliness found, so life does spin,
The secret to living is letting jokes in.

A Journey Through Time's Garden

In a garden where clocks grow like vines,
Every tick-tock jests and twines.
Flowers bloom at curious rates,
Inviting giggles with silly traits.

Sunflowers turning with a grin,
Chasing light, as laughter spins.
The daisies muddle thoughts of haste,
Sowing wrinkles of smile with taste.

Juggling time, the weeds and blooms,
Dance with mischief in the glooms.
A rabbit hops with a watch in paw,
Exclaims, "Oh dear! Who set this law?"

Through twists and turns, we laugh and play,
The garden's charm keeps worries at bay.
For in this patch where humor sways,
Time grows soft, as joy displays.

The Embrace of Silent Growth

In the quiet soil, worms have fun,
Digging tunnels, they're never done.
While roots stretch deep with giggles low,
Branches shake with a silent show.

Caterpillars munch with glee on leaves,
Tickling plants with silly sleeves.
A secret joke the trees all know,
That growth can dance, even slow.

Silent whispers weave through the air,
As nature chuckles without a care.
Each sprout rejoices in its way,
For growth can bring a jolly play.

So celebrate the secrets of the ground,
Where laughter and stillness swirl around.
For in that hush, the fun surprises,
Quiet growth brings out the best disguises.

The Barometer of Soft Wishes

A barometer swings with wishes bright,
Measuring dreams in the soft moonlight.
Each gentle sway, a hope or jest,
Up goes the laughter; down goes the rest.

Whispers float like feathers in flight,
Tickling clouds with pure delight.
A wish for cookies, a wish for more,
The scale of joy goes to the core.

Winds of change bring breezy tales,
With sails of hope, we ride the gales.
Weathering storms of silly schemes,
Finding humor stitched in dreams.

So let's take turns, wish and cheer,
Twirling with laughter that draws us near.
For in the dance of soft desires,
We light the world with spark and fires.

The Patience of Morning Dew

In the morning, droplets cling,
Waiting for the sun to spring.
They giggle as they slowly slide,
Off a leaf on nature's ride.

The ants march by, in single file,
They stop to chat, and stay awhile.
"Hey there, buddy, where's the rush?"
"I'm just soaking, in a hush."

Along comes wind, with a cheeky tease,
"Come on, dudes, move with the breeze!"
But dew just winks, and stays put tight,
"I'm not ready, quite the sight!"

So if you see them, don't despair,
Waiting's fun when and if you dare.
Laughter drips from every leaf,
A funny tale, beyond belief.

As the Garden Breathes

In a garden full of cheer,
Plants are dancing, loud and clear.
A daisy jig, a rose's twirl,
Watch them laugh, they dance and whirl.

"Why so glum?" asks leafy sage,
A beetle frowns, not to engage.
"Just waiting for my turn to bloom,"
"Cheer up, pal, it's not your doom!"

A squirrel sidles in, quite spry,
"Join the fun, don't be shy!"
"Life's too short to sulk and pout,"
He somersaults, turning about.

So, if you're stuck in waiting room,
Think of flowers, how they bloom.
Each moment is a silly chance,
To join the garden's merry dance!

Gentle Unraveling of Time

A clock ticks slow, quite out of tune,
It hummed along since it was noon.
"Twelve again?" it starts to fret,
"Oh dear, this is a wild duet!"

The seconds giggle, roll around,
"Let's play hide and seek, no need to frown!"
Minutes twirl, then take a leap,
Falling softly, into sleep.

"Is it lunchtime yet?" the hour sighs,
As crumbs from toast dance 'neath the skies.
"I'll cook spaghetti, with a twist,
However long, it can't be missed!"

So laughter lingers in that space,
A gentle game of time and grace.
As minutes giggle, tick and tease,
It's all a jest, so take it with ease!

The Harmony of Earth and Sky

Look up high, the clouds are laughing,
Swirling round, their shapes are drafting.
A cow that floats, a whale that soars,
Nature's jest, come hear the roars.

Below, the grass is in a jest,
Pretending that it's on a quest.
"Who am I? Where do I go?"
The soil chuckles, "Just take it slow!"

Birds swoop down, a comic dive,
Chasing clouds, they feel alive.
"Got your wings? Let's see you fly!"
The sky retorts, "Or at least try!"

So join the fun, both earth and air,
With laughter floating everywhere.
In this silly dance we all partake,
United in jokes that nature makes.

Surrendering to the Breeze

A dandelion dreams of flight,
But here it sits, still and slight.
It sneezes loud on a sunny day,
Blowing dreams that drift away.

The wind laughs back, a cheeky friend,
Covering faces, to no end.
A twirl, a swirl, as it slides by,
The flower's sigh, a popcorn high.

Garden gnomes brace for surprise,
As petals dance before their eyes.
With every gust, they spin around,
In nature's circus, giggles abound.

But aimless flight needs some finesse,
Not all balloons float, I confess.
Yet in this mess, a charm we find,
In each blown kiss, laughter entwined.

Silent Moments in the Petal Rain

Raindrops drip like soft applause,
Dancing on leaves without a pause.
Each drop a joke the flowers share,
While bees buzz by without a care.

It's a comedy show on a green stage,
With petals as actors, wise and sage.
A sunflower winks, oh so bright,
While tulips giggle in sheer delight.

The earth listens with bated breath,
As laughter blooms beyond sweet death.
Silence breaks, a chuckle swells,
A row of daisies ring the bells.

In this garden, jokes unfurl,
Life's a jest, a curious whirl.
With every petal that takes a dive,
The joy of nature, so alive.

Where Time Meets Tender Blossoms

A clock tick-tocks with gentle grace,
While blossoms giggle, keeping pace.
Each petal whispers, "What's the rush?"
As squirrels chase tails in a silly hush.

Time wears a hat that's far too grand,
While flowers dance on shifting sand.
They plot their moves, a subtle game,
To avoid the bee that's lost its name.

The sun peeks in with a playful wink,
As blossoms gather for a drink.
A bee proposes, "Let's be bold!"
While buttercups laugh, their stories told.

In the garden of laughs, time's a jest,
Where every moment feels like a fest.
Together they bloom, so wise and bright,
In a timeless dance, pure delight.

In the Shade of a Careful Heart

Under the leaves, a secret keeps,
A giggling gnome as the sunlight peeps.
He whispers soft to the flowers near,
"Don't take life so seriously, my dear!"

With every shadow, a tickle finds,
As nature plays its sly designs.
Between the giggles and buzzing chats,
The heart of the garden stumbles at that.

Daisies erupt with joy and jest,
Making the evening quite the fest.
While bumblebees join in the fun,
The careful heart beats as one.

Laughter echoes beneath the boughs,
Where secrets flourish and wonder vows.
In the shade, the humor starts,
Cradled softly by careful hearts.

Petal Journeys Through Time

In a garden where socks often stray,
A flower decided to roll in the hay.
It danced with a bee, wearing a crown,
While butterflies giggled at the sight of a frown.

"Oh dear, what a mess!" the tulip declared,
As the flowers around began to be scared.
With petals a-flutter and pollen amiss,
They chalked it up to a very odd bliss.

The sun peeked in, wearing shades of bright gold,
While the daisies whispered, "This story is bold!"
The roses, though jealous, couldn't keep straight,
How a flower could frolic and still be late.

A snail on a leaf gave a slow, steady nod,
"Time's just a trick, my dear friends, it's a fraud!"
With a wink and a smile, he uncoiled his shell,
And told them of secrets he learned from a bell.

Then the petals all laughed, and the garden took flight,
In a whirl of bouquets that danced through the night.
With giggles and joy, they forgot all their fuss,
Because laughter, it seems, is a must for all of us.

Unveiling the Silent Bloom

In the hush of the night, a bloom had an itch,
It whispered to stars, "Oh, isn't this rich?"
The daffodils chuckled, with petals a-wag,
Inventing new tales of their favorite rag.

A ladybug paused to inspect the decor,
"Are these blooms having parties, or is this folklore?"
The tulip replied, while perched on a vine,
"It's all just a ploy to make gardens divine!"

The lilies all snickered, as they practiced their winks,
While the daisies plotted their next clever prinks.
Behind every bloom there's a tale or a quirk,
And flowers, it seems, are good at their work!

So as they all danced in moonlight's sweet thrill,
They declared there's no hurry, they had time to kill.
With petals a-flutter, a sight to be seen,
Unveiling the laughter where silence had been.

Whispers of Blooming Silence

In the garden's arena, the flowers conspired,
The sun gave a wink while the clouds felt inspired.
A violet proclaimed, through a giggle and sway,
"Let's start a performance; we'll steal the whole day!"

The roses rolled eyes, like, "What do you mean?"
But deep down, they secretly wanted to preen.
As petals took stage, they showed off their flair,
With much ado, the whole garden did stare!

A bumblebee buzzed, gave them nods of approval,
As a rogue wind declared, "This show is so jewel!"
The daisies performed in their sunny, bright hues,
While the tulips broke out into old-fashioned blues.

The evening colored their whispers with glee,
Where flowers wore laughter as bright as could be.
In the silent abode where nature did thrive,
They found joy in the stillness, and felt so alive.

The Art of Waiting Blossoms

In a meadow of dreams, where time took a stroll,
The blooms waited patiently, as if on a roll.
A poppy sighed gently, "Is this a good plan?"
While a nearby daisy said, "I'm so much more glam!"

They counted the seconds like kids play a game,
Where waiting was part of their intricate fame.
"I'll wait for the rain!" the rose yelled with glee,
As the others debated who'd weather the spree.

Then a squirrel popped by, in a nutty ballet,
"Waiting's like dancing; you just sway and play!"
With a jump and a twirl, he made quite the scene,
As blossoms erupted in fits of bright green.

Together they laughed, at the fuss about time,
In the art of just waiting, they found a grand rhyme.
With colors and giggles, they bloomed side by side,
Creating a canvas where fun could abide.

Seasons of Slow Unfolding

In springtime's giggle, buds do tease,
They take their time like a lazy breeze.
With every sunny, bright-eyed morn,
They yawn and stretch, 'I'm not yet born!'

The summer shines, they play peek-a-boo,
While bees bumble by, like they've lost their queue.
'Come join the party!' the daisies shout,
But still, some are snoozing, having no doubt.

Autumn's dance makes the branches sway,
'Time to show colors!' they cheerfully say.
But have you seen how long it takes?
They finish their meal, while the squirrel fakes.

Winter arrives with a chilly grin,
The buds all sigh, 'Oh, let us in!'
They'd rather wait for a sunny day,
'Until then, let's nap and dream away!'

A Tapestry of Quiet Growth

In the garden's hum, worms make their beds,
Who needs a rush? They have dreams instead.
Seeds inch slowly, like a snail parade,
Mystified by the endless charade.

Leaves whisper gossip, behind the sun's glare,
'Have you seen how the trees comb their hair?'
They don't mind the wait, it's part of the fun,
The more time to shade from the midday sun.

Roots send secret texts, deep underground,
Amusing themselves where no one's around.
'Oh, look at the tulips, they think they're cool!'
While dandelions giggle, 'This is our school!'

Patience is savvy, it knows how to tease,
While nature's at play, just let it appease.
In time's gentle grasp, life learns to embrace,
A tapestry woven in a slow, sly grace.

The Art of Waiting in Bloom

A flower's dream starts with a chuckle,
As it waits for bees, it begins to huddle.
'Why hurry at all?' it asks the bud,
'There's snacks to enjoy, like earth's rich mud!'

Comfy in soil, with a cozy shout,
They plan their takeoff, from a tiny sprout.
'Let's hold a meeting, under the moon!
We'll get there, but hey, let's snooze till noon!'

The sun peeks out, the blossoms all grin,
'Oh, look who's here! Let's start the spin!'
In a wiggly dance, they swirl without care,
Why rush to bloom when there's laughter to share?

The waiting itself turns into a game,
Everyone chuckling, it's never the same.
Life's too short for a hurry or fuss,
The art of stillness brings blossoms to us.

Beneath the Flowering Sky

The clouds above play a game of hide,
Sun peeks through, like a kid's wild ride.
Flowers below say, 'What's the fuss?'
We'll burst through soon, don't make a fuss!

In a daisy's world, patience is key,
'Let's tell the world how fun it can be.'
With silly puns and whimsical chime,
They all bide their time; it's blooming prime!

Buds debate, with a chuckling tone,
'Is it my turn to take the throne?'
But like good friends, they'll wait in line,
For each little bloom is a stroke divine.

As twilight comes, the petals ascend,
Mocking the hurry, and time they suspend.
The sky watches on with a joyful sigh,
In a world of waiting, they love to fly!

In the Embrace of Tender Delays

A turtle wears a tiny hat,
In his world, it's all about that.
While the rabbit races like the wind,
The party's on, but he ain't pinned.

With every step, he stops to snack,
Savoring the moments, no need to rush back.
The crowd's all waiting, toes a-tapping,
"Hey tortoise, just stop with the napping!"

The finish line is a distant joke,
He waves to his fans, shares a poke.
With each slow waddle, laughter spreads,
While the hare's still dreaming in his snug beds.

So here's to the hustle, the race, the chase,
But slower paces have their grace.
In the end, with laughter overlaid,
Not every party needs a parade.

Easing Into the Sunlit Dawn

The rooster's snooze alarm rings late,
"Just five more minutes... isn't that great?"
He dreams of worms and sunny skies,
While the farmer grumbles, eyes in a surprise.

Outside, the cow's in a yoga pose,
"Why must we rush? I must decompose!"
The sheep all giggle, jumping the fence,
In this sleepy town, common sense makes no sense.

A snail dreams of speed and running around,
In this world, he's quite renowned.
"Patience," he tells the sprightly hare,
"Today, we'll take time, life's a fair!"

The sun emerges, yawning so wide,
The rooster's anger comes on a slide.
But as they gather for coffee and toast,
They laugh through the morning, and that's what counts most.

Petal by Petal: The Promise of Tomorrow

A flower wishes it could sing,
But pollen sneezes ruin the fling.
So it dances cheeky in the breeze,
Mocking raindrops with leafy tease.

The bee is lazy, sipping tea,
"Why do I buzz when I could just be?"
It's hard to work with a sunny grin,
And nothing says "nap" like a light spin.

The sun overhears their merry plight,
And beams with humor, feeling quite bright.
"Well, if you're waiting for blooms to rise,
Just make sure to enjoy the skies!"

Tomorrow's promise is more of the same,
With each tiny bloom, they rejoice in the game.
For laughter grows wild, like weeds in the field,
Where joy's the harvest, and none shall yield.

When Dreams Root in Soft Earth

A dreamer plants his wish with care,
"Grow fast!" he shouts, "Let's go somewhere!"
But seeds laugh back and slowly sink,
"Chill a bit mate, let's rethink."

The moon's now giggling, hiding behind,
At the gardener's frantic, wiggly grind.
"Roots take time, you silly fool,
Just put down your spade, it's nature's rule."

Worms come out with tiny applause,
"Hold your horses, no need for a cause!"
As he waits, the blossoms share a drink,
In the soft earth, they all happily link.

So here's to the waiting, the giggles, the cheer,
For dreams will pop up, just give them a year!
In the embrace of soil, love and mirth,
We find joy in the patience of the earth.

Soft Echoes of Growth

In a garden where daisies all chatter,
A snail once claimed, 'I'm a fast-top sprinter!'
But with his slow speed, he'd soon lose the race,
While laughing flowers threw him a dance space.

Bees wear tuxedos to buzz in a line,
While worms in their evening gowns shine so fine.
The sun winks shyly, refusing to show,
As ants tell tall stories of the seeds they sow.

A gust of the breeze starts a leafy debate,
Who's the tallest, the lettuce, or this pine plate?
The veggies mock carrots for wearing a coat,
While sprouts play charades, keepin' things afloat.

But here we stand, with our green-thumbed flair,
Each bloom and each joke lightens up the air.
So break out the laughter, let worries all cease,
In nature's wild circus, we dance for our peace.

The Dance of Fragile Hues

A butterfly slid, all elegant and neat,
On a flower that told jokes, oh so sweet.
The petals giggled in colors so bright,
While grumpy old cacti weren't feeling the light.

In the breeze, the tulips began a parade,
The daisies danced 'round, in sunshine they played.
A ladybug blushed, being spotted so well,
And teased by the blooms; 'Hey, who's that bell?

The sunflowers stood tall, like they owned the day,
While gossamer spiders spun dreams in their way.
A dance-off erupted, no time to be shy,
With blooms spinning round, even moths gave a try.

But as night fell, they tucked in with glee,
Whispering tales of their day, wild and free.
In bright-colored dreams, they would meet once again,
To recreate laughter, forever our friend.

Blossoms Amidst the Shadows

In the dark of the night, the blossoms would giggle,
With moonlight as spotlight, they'd wriggle and wiggle.
A raccoon named Fred joined the floral ballet,
While shadows all chuckled, enjoying the play.

The roses wore crowns that were far too tight,
Complaining to violets about their plight.
But the daisies laughed on, saying 'Fret not,'
For who most likely shows off, the blooms or the plot?

A fox took a selfie, but forgot how to pose,
While every sweet petal began to take those woes.
'Let's bloom like we mean it!', the daisies all cried,
With faces of bliss while giggling wide-eyed.

So amidst all the shadows, they bloomed and they joked,
Creating a space where all worries were poked.
For in the garden's realm, under starlit domains,
Even in silence, the laughter remains.

Seasons of Subtle Resilience

In springtime, the daisies wore hats made of dew,
While frogs in their blazers joined in for the view.
With sunshine as humor, they basked in their prime,
Telling tales of last winter, oh so sublime.

As summer arrived, with its warmth and delight,
The flowers exchanged nicknames with gentle insight.
A sunflower named Sally sang karaoke, all day,
While pansies performed in their theatrical play.

When autumn crept in, armed with crisp, chilly air,
The leaves gave a dance-off, oh what a fair!
As crickets serenaded, the blooms took their stand,
Challenging pumpkin spice with a wink and a hand.

And when winter rolled in, with snowflakes to boast,
The flowers dipped down, but never did they coast.
With patience and laughter, they waited their cue,
For spring would return, bringing life anew.

www.ingramcontent.com/pod-product-compliance
Lightning Source LLC
Chambersburg PA
CBHW070319120526
44590CB00017B/2742